By Tony Drury
May 2011

Goodbye Dave
My decision to leave the Conservative Party

David Cameron and Tony Drury were still together in 2006. It was not to last ...

London 6th November 2006

Published by EntBrit Ltd in May 2011

Tony Drury has asserted his rights under the Copyright, Designs and Patents Act 1988, to be identified as author of this book.

Copyright © 2011 Tony Drury. All rights reserved.

ISBN: 978-1-4476-6854-1

No part of this book may be reproduced in any form without the express permission from the publisher except for the quotation of brief passages in reviews.

Please contact Enterprise Britain for more information at
mail@enterprisebritain.com.

Contents

I - The Beginning of the End..4
II - Local Politics 21
III - Change of Leader: Iain Duncan Smith and Michael Howard 30
IV - Lord Lamont and Lord Flight..38
V - The Blue Dragon Club 48
VI - David Cameron, Andrew Mackay and Julie Kirkbride...........63
VII - Enterprise Britain and Mr. Angry.......................................75
Index...77

This book is dedicated to those democratic citizens who believe in a meritocracy promoting the creation and fair distribution of wealth.

I - The Beginning of the End

"They are bloody users, Tone".

I am Tone: usually Tony. But 'Tone' is what my friend Robert Boot calls me.

My actual Christian name is Anthony. Early on in my life I discovered that it means 'praiseworthy'. As I was already slightly rebellious, I changed it to 'Tony'.

Robert Boot is a fine man. He is happily married. This is, in part, because he chose well but also because Christine, his wife, is a divorce lawyer and he knows how much straying can cost.

Robert smiled a smile. "They always have been and they always will be" he summarised.

'They' were the Conservative Party of Great Britain. Perhaps more pertinently 'they' were the Coalition Government led by a power crazed Old Etonian.

I was in despair. My politics over the preceding twenty five years had been with the Conservative Party. I had been a Constituency Chairman (South West Bedfordshire), a Bedfordshire County Councillor, a rejected Parliamentary Candidate, and Chairman of The Blue Dragon Club (the Welsh Conservatives in London).

I had wined and dined MPs and members of the Upper House. I regularly went to the Carlton Club in St. James's and dined with Party officials at Wiltons, the 'Conservative' restaurant in Jermyn Street.

A Personal Confession

My political career, however, was impeded by one situation. I was not, and am not, wealthy.

By many people's standards I have done well. We have a lovely home in a woodland area of Leighton Buzzard in Bedfordshire and a holiday home in Aberdovey, Wales. I drive a Mercedes. However much of this has been achieved on borrowed money and, not unlike a former Conservative Prime Minister, I have spent periods of my life struggling to balance the books.

"Even as he took office as Chancellor, on 28 February 1852, Philip Rose had to lend him £1,500 to tide him over, while a fortnight later Hobhouse (now Lord Broughton) recorded in his diary that there were rumours that the new Chancellor was in great pecuniary difficulties..." ('Disraeli' by Sarah Bradford: 1996: Phoenix)

You can fool some people too easily. In 2003, when I was a Bedfordshire County Councillor for Plantation Ward in Leighton Buzzard, and during a morning session in the Council chambers, I was following my favourite pastime of baiting the Liberal Democrats. We had a strict whip so I could rarely contribute to political banter for fear of upsetting Councillor Angela Roberts the formidable Conservative leader.

We were debating traffic congestion in Leighton Buzzard and I had pounced on a weak proposal from the Liberal Democrats. Such was the impact of my rhetoric that I managed to create a temporary coalition of Liberal Democrats and Labour (Nick Clegg could learn from me: I achieved the right one). The merits of the proposal had long gone and the exchanges had become personal. A Labour Councillor struck, fatally.

"Chairman" he exclaimed. *"How can Councillor Drury even begin to understand what the people of Leighton Buzzard are suffering trying to get to work on our congested roads when he is driving his luxury car around the leafy lanes of Plantation Road where he lives."*

Ouch. Good point. I decided to vote against myself.

Parliamentary Candidate?

At one point in the late 1990s I thought I was ready to progress my political career. My company, St. Helen's Capital, a corporate finance house based in the City of London, was prospering. We specialised in raising capital for 'smaller' companies and this was the period of 'dot com' riches.

I became a County Councillor in Bedfordshire in 2001 and was politically ambitious. I soon made my first, and only, attempt at becoming a Member of Parliament although in somewhat unexpected circumstances.

In early 2000 our sitting MP, Sir David Madel, announced his retirement. I was then Chairman of South West Bedfordshire Conservative Association and began working with Area officials on the selection of the Prospective Parliamentary Candidate ("PPC").

We had a particularly strong committee including a number of Dunstable and Leighton Buzzard Parish, Town, District and County Councillors. Our President, Sir Neville Bowman-Shaw, had his palatial Toddington Manor home near to Junction 12 of the M1. Sir Neville was rebuilding his life after the sale of his business, Lancer Boss Group, to the Germans.

My phone rang and I was asked to attend a meeting of the Committee. This took place a few nights later. Their message was simple. I was a good guy and they wanted me to stand for selection as their PPC. I was dumbstruck.

The next two weeks were hectic. I met with Sir David who gave me some thoughtful advice. I visited Sir Peter Brown, who was John Major's agent, and now the Area boss. We had always maintained a good relationship. I discussed several personal issues with Sir Peter and obtained his agreement that I should stand.

It is hard work to become a parliamentary candidate for the Conservatives unless you went to Eton and you are a friend of David Cameron. There is a rigorous selection process which is the filter to the Candidate list. Once on that you can apply for any vacancy which arises. You will usually be one of many.

There is an exception to that system. A local candidate can enter if agreed by the Area officials.

I called a meeting of the Board of Directors of St. Helen's Capital and, much to my surprise, they backed my candidacy. The senior non-executive director said that it would bring honour to the company.

An envelope arrived and I was told to attend the first selection meeting on the following Sunday at 10.00am at a Primary School in Dunstable.

The morning came and I was nervous. I arrived at the school and after thirty minutes I was called in to the assembly hall. There was a desk and chair. Sitting around, somewhat in the dark, was a horseshoe of local members. I remember thinking that it was similar to the interrogation of the OAS terrorist in the film 'The Day of the Jackal'. I waited for the electric shocks to come surging through my limbs.

The first part was a ten minute presentation wherein I set out my credentials. I was poor but far worse was to follow. I faced a barrage of questions. The nadir came when the aforementioned Councillor Angela Roberts asked me whether the provisions of the 1948 Education Act could contribute to teaching standards in Bedfordshire.

The correct answer should have been:

"That is an outstanding question Councillor Roberts for which I thank you. Education will always be my number one priority as it is yours. However I cannot do it alone. I will want to work with the experts. Your outstanding knowledge and achievements in the field of education will be my bedrock for building a future that secures for the youngsters of Bedfordshire the best standards possible."

My actual answer was:

"I really think that is a ridiculous question. I want to talk about the economy."

Later that evening a rather hesitant member of the Committee telephoned me to say what a huge impression I had made. Unfortunately there were a number of outstanding candidates and I would not be required for the second round of interviews.

I beat myself up for several weeks. I vowed to return a more fluent and competent candidate in the future. But I was never to get the opportunity. I returned to the day job and my work as a County Councillor.

At this time, the main Director at St. Helen's Capital, in London was a wealthy Old Harrovian, whose family own a village in South Yorkshire. Despite his personal qualities, in my opinion he needed additional executive support if we were to maximise the potential of the growing business. I felt compelled to resign as a County Councillor and to return to the City. This I did.

St. Helen's Capital prospered and became the leading PLUS-quoted corporate finance advisory firm. In 2006 I ceased full time working and sold my shares. I thought I had broken through the debt barrier and, with five non-executive directorships already agreed, was looking forward to next stage of my career. I was underprovided on pension but I hoped to create further wealth through my shareholdings.

The recession began in 2007 and within two years I was plunged into debt again. The small-cap sector was hit badly and I lost four of my directorships as companies delisted from the markets. As I write I am just coming out of a four year battle to avoid selling the house(s).

The Party's donor

It is therefore all the more remarkable that by my calculations I have been a consistent donor to the Conservative Party.

If I add up the sums I have spent on dinners, raffles, membership fees, the various Central Office wheezes to collect money (I was at one time paying £5,000 annually to be a member of the Front Bench Club) and latterly to the Blue Dragon Club, I calculate it to be around £43,000.

In many ways this was contributory to my decision to cease being a member of a Conservative Party of which David Cameron is leader.

The main reasons which drove me to my decision were:

- Dave had lost an Election he should have won hands down

- Our renewal membership of South West Bedfordshire, £50, was due. I asked Judy, my wife: "Do you want to give Dave another £50?" "No" she said. Dave had just taken £1million off David Rowland who we, in the City, know of quite well. I actually knew his son better. Dad, "Spotty" Rowland, was not my type of Conservative and I was appalled that Cameron had taken his money. In January 2011 David Rowland was again in the news when he lost an appeal at the Luxembourg Supreme Court. He was trying to keep documents, linked to an Icelandic financial investigation, private. There is no suggestion of any wrongdoing by David Rowland. By March 2011 the situation had deteriorated further when Prince Andrew, following damaging revelations about his connections with Libya, tried to distance himself from David Rowland

- I never could agree to Coalition Government. David Cameron could, and should, have gone for minority Government and stayed true to Conservative principles.

- Following the election result events moved quickly. I was baffled that the Conservatives should consider Coalition with the Liberal Democrats, disagreed with it at every stage and have watched subsequent developments with horror.

- I became concerned that David Cameron's driving motivation was his desire for personal ego and power. The reason he lost the 2010 General Election was because he was responsible for a political manifesto which lacked well expressed Conservative principles.

- No sooner had he taken office than he was grabbing headlines with ill thought through statements:
    - July 2010: we were junior partners to the Americans in World War Two
    - July 2010: Pakistan must not be allowed to promote export of terror
    - October 2010: the EU will not be allowed any budget increase (the officials ran rings round him and increased the budget anyway)
    - February 2011: Big Society is here to stay
    - April 2011: failing to reform the NHS will 'end in tears'
    - and so on.

- The activities of his personal advisers, Steve Hilton, and others appalled me. The Cameron fan club, Policy Exchange, was exacting far too much influence. His personal backing of Andy Coulson, even at the time of the Election, was an unnecessary risk (good Public School habit, of course, personal loyalty). As the phone tapping episode has developed, Cameron's judgement looks increasingly misplaced.

- Nick Boles, the MP for Grantham and Stamford, the founder of Policy Exchange, and a close friend of David Cameron, had an article in 'The Times' on 13 September 2010 arguing the case for a Coalition Manifesto in 2015. I suspected that Cameron agreed to the publication of this article.

In summary, I revisited my growing beliefs that David Cameron lacked political depth and was driven by his personal lust for power. He was willing to ditch genuine Conservative principles by forging an alliance with a Party which occupies a completely different political sector. Before the 2010 Election result was known, informed commentators were anticipating a possible link between Labour and the Liberal Democrats.

Within a few weeks of taking office it was clear that David Cameron was a Liberal Conservative and was being influenced, in particular, by Nick Boles and Policy Exchange. Early in his term he tried to neutralise the power of the 1922 Conservative Backbench Committee because he knew that is from where the opposition would emanate.

What depressed me more was that few people seem to realise what was happening.

I did! I exercised my right to protest by not renewing my membership of the Conservative Party.

Lunch with the Right Honourable Cheryl Gillan

The point at which Robert confirmed my worst fears, *"they are bloody users, Tone"*, was in early September 2010.

On 7 September I entertained at lunch The Right Honourable Cheryl Gillan MP, Secretary of State for Wales. I knew Cheryl, the MP for Chesham and Amersham (which upsets many of the Welsh voters), rather well and, over the years, she had accepted a number of invitations from me.

We usually had fun. I had a long standing and deep respect for her. She had suffered ill health and was a woman of courage. She struggled, as Opposition spokesperson in the House of Commons, with Peter Hain, the Welsh Secretary, during the latter part of the Labour Government, who was (and remains) a political bruiser.

In a TV debate involving Party leaders in Wales during the Election Campaign, Cheryl had referred to the Labour Leader as Rhodri Morgan. He had relinquished this post several months earlier and Hain pounced. Cheryl was un-necessarily upset and we exchanged emails.

The Conservative Welsh Assembly leader, Nick Bourne, seemed to take over and did rather well. There were rumours that Cheryl might not get the Welsh job especially as in Cardiff North, the former MEP and charismatic Jonathan Evans had won and would be entering the House of Commons. David Jones MP for Clwyd West was another strong contender.

The Conservatives won eight seats in Wales in the General Election, out of forty, an increase of five. The Welsh Conservatives were ecstatic. The truth was that a year earlier Cheryl and Dave had agreed a target of thirteen. Dave lost those seats because he allowed the Party to fight the Election without a meaningful manifesto.

I was excited about seeing Cheryl. I had been required to adapt to dealing with the Welsh Office and it was hard work. They cancelled me twice but the day came. We met at Wiltons just before 1.00pm.

"I have to go at ten past two" she opened and I thought that she seemed tense.

I was with a Cabinet Minister. I was on my best behaviour. I wanted to entertain her properly.

I tried to discuss the potential for a Welsh Stock Exchange. I had written a paper on the subject. Regional Exchanges struggle to work in the modern financial environment. This is because since 1986 and 'Big Bang', electronic trading rules financial services. However I was aware of some potentially sizable backing in Wales. I therefore created a model that might work.

"I have already been advised by my officials," said Cheryl. "They don't work." That was the end of that part of our conversation.

She then asked, somewhat to my surprise, what I was doing for the economy of Wales. Our conversation stuttered along in this context. This was not the Cheryl Gillan I recognised from a number of years of working together.

It felt like a Cabinet meeting to me. I could almost hear David Cameron lecturing his ministers: "It's all Labour's fault."

"I really think I have some ideas Cheryl" I mumbled although she had now moved on to her main course.

The lunch reached its painful ending and off she went.

I felt as though I had received a Cameron public school dressing down.

The final event

My walk out of Jermyn Street in Mayfair and down St. James's was personally painful. I felt that I had been 'put down'. I did not like it and I did not think I deserved it.

That evening, The Blue Dragons held a reception at the Carlton Club for the Welsh Conservative Members of Parliaments including the five new MPs. I had found a sponsor from the City. He was so appalled by the early days of the Coalition Government, he withdrew his support. The previous year I had spent nearly £4,000 supporting the Club. This comprised taking three tables at the 2009 annual dinner, committee meeting rooms and starting to pay the Administrator £125 per month.

I knew I had no choice but to pay around £1,200 to fund the evening. The organisation had been frustrating. The Government closed down in August and nobody responded to emails. To avoid a failure I pulled in some friends so that the Cabinet Room, in the basement of the Club, was full. Of the eight Welsh MPs, four came. Only three had replied. I had sent an email to David Jones MP, the leader of the Welsh Conservatives in Westminster, with whom I had a good relationship. I told him of the lack of response but it seemed to have no effect.

Cheryl was the guest of honour and spoke rather well. I had given her a Drury special by way of an introduction and she had loved it. The evening was a success.

Political emotions

Overnight I lay awake and reflected on a conversation I had shared with my sister, Gill, a few weeks earlier. I am still not sure whether she and her husband Tim (an utterly decent man) vote, or have voted, Liberal Democrat and/or Labour over the years. What I do know is that Gill literally hates the Conservatives and at one point, when I was at my Thatcherite regal best, I was banned from mentioning the Conservatives in her home.

Over the last few years Gill and I have become rather close. She is incredibly active and talented. She has been an amateur actor of great achievement and a Thespian director. She has a huge social conscience and is a prison visitor. She abhors racism.

We were spending a Sunday having lunch at their Farnham home. Tim was barbecuing and Judy was drinking white wine and they were talking. Gill was showing interest in my political views especially as I was already formulating and expressing my concerns over David Cameron.

"You know Gill" I said. "I am not sure I am really a Conservative. Yes, I believe passionately in wealth creation but I also want a meritocracy. I want wealth distributed much more evenly."

I faced my sister. "Gill" I said. "Cameron is everything with which I struggle. He is filthy rich and has a public school superiority which I find so false."

Gill looked at me. "Ant" (my family name). "Ant" she smiled. "I have always thought that you are not truly a Conservative." We returned home but I could not sleep. I went in to my study and took out a paper I had written in the autumn.

It was headed 'The enemy within: the inside story of the catastrophic ownership of the Conservative Party by the fabulously rich, land owning public school educated cabal.'

The Etonian question

It had been written as a result of a session I had spent with my son-in-law Simon.

Simon is a fascinating man. He is also a great husband to my daughter Emma who is registered blind. Simon had given up being Head of Business Studies at Trinity Academy in Doncaster and qualified as a barrister. It nearly broke his health but the ceremony at Gray's Inn in the summer of 2010 had made it all worthwhile. He was highly placed in his examinations.

He could not get a pupillage and he needed work. He was up to his eyes in debt with student loans. He had made a legal friend from a land-owning family in the north. Simon kept coming second in his interviews. His friend had told him that he lacked Eton and Oxbridge. My hackles were raised.

Twenty British Prime Ministers were educated at Eton. They include Robert Walpole, William Pitt the Elder, Gladstone, Sir Anthony Eden,

Gray's Inn 22 July 2010: my son-in-law becomes a barrister

Harold Macmillan, Sir Alex Douglas-Home and, of course, David Cameron. Alexander Boris de Pfeffel Johnson went to Eton.

My own MP Andrew Selous was educated at Eton but somehow it never seemed an issue.

My position has always been that it is an issue of individual merit. As someone who believes in wealth creation, there will always be division in society. Social mobility is an ongoing issue. Most people do not want to improve outside their social class. I also recognise that a number of Britain's public schools are actively broadening their intake.

However, my concern is that positions in the Conservative Party and in the Civil Service remain dominated by wealth and educational background. The Labour Party of 1997 was more representative of Britain.

My sleeplessness continued. I called the dog ('Summer') and we drove to the lakes at Caldecott, south of Milton Keynes. We completed our one hour's walk around the waters. The birdsong was inspirational. There were, at that time, four heron on the south stretch. Their wingspans were amazing as they took off to feed. As we reached the car Summer wagged her tail. She knew that Judy would have prepared her breakfast ready for her on our return home. My mind was made up.

Later in my London office Robert Boot listened to my outburst as I released my frustrations.

"Robert," I said. "I can't join another Party. I'm a Conservative. I'll be a floating voter."

"They are bloody users, Tone," said Robert. "They want you for your money."

I wrote at some length to Andrew Selous who was, and is, the member for South West Bedfordshire. I later received a thoughtful reply from Andrew.

Judy said to me: "Tony. I must vote for Andrew. He is a wonderful MP." I felt exactly the same way.

I wrote to Michael Howard whom I had just persuaded to become President of the Blue Dragon Club in succession to the late Lord (Peter) Walker. My final email was to Andrew Mackay and Julie Kirkbride the former Conservative MPs.

The Blue Dragon Club

The full story of the three years, during which I was chairman of the Blue Dragon Club, is told in Chapter Five.

I was determined to go quietly. The Club was proving a success and I did not want to derail it. In this I succeeded. Simon Mort took over as Acting Chairman and proved splendidly efficient. His 2010 Annual Dinner at the Cavalry & Guards Club in Piccadilly was financially profitable and gave a boost to the funding of the Welsh 2011 Assembly election campaign.

My letter of resignation highlighted my growing business responsibilities. After nearly four years of struggling (I am never sure what George Osborne had been doing but my recession began in 2007) my fortunes were changing. I had been invited to take the chair of a London based corporate finance house. I was approved by the Financial Services Authority and began work.

During the summer of 2010 I was invited to visit a Chinese company with an exciting internet product. I subsequently travelled to Guangzhou, which is two hours north of Shenzhen, just across the border from Hong Kong. I met with the Chinese chief executive, Jin Jin Leune, a youthful entrepreneur. Her English name is Jessie. She and I started a good business relationship.

The picture shows Jessie hosting a lunch following our business presentations. I am sitting to her left. On her right is Nicholas Littlewood, an experienced US and UK investment banker. He is Chairman of Ford Eagle Group, a China and Hong Kong based corporate finance house. We were, and

At lunch with Jin Jin Jeune at Guangzhou

are, working together to bring Chinese businesses to the London markets. During the lunch I managed a diplomatic incident.

China culture meant that all those at the lunch table were respecting Jessie's position as the Founder and Chief Executive of the business. Jessie held court. As I was a visitor I also was so honoured.

Jessie's English was not too bad but we were using an interpreter. She was telling me about her family background, her education in China, Singapore and Sydney University. She had spent two years in Australia obtaining her MBA. I thought things were going rather well.

It made sense to me at the time but I asked Jessie if she had a bike. My thinking was that she was a 'modern' woman and I guessed she would go to a gym or ride around the streets as they do in London.

I was told later that when it was translated into Chinese it came out as "Are you a migrant worker?"

We recovered but I should have thought more carefully. Who rides the millions of bikes in China?

David Cameron seems prone to making statements which are ill thought through. At Davos (January 2011) he advised against investing in Chinese companies. Does he have no idea how hard some of us work to develop our foreign contacts?

In March 2011, my company signed contracts with Jessie's Board of Directors to introduce her business to the London Stock Exchange.

I resigned as Chairman of the Blue Dragon Club citing business commitments.

The Presentation that went away

Quite early on I was told that the Committee wanted to make a presentation to me at the annual dinner. I resisted because I thought it was not necessary. They persisted and I agreed to book a table. I invited a number of City contacts.

The night of the dinner came during an awful early December cold spell and it was a labour of love to reach the Cavalry & Guards Club. We had a great table. I had written to my guests explaining that there would be a presentation to me during the evening. If anybody could not face hearing nice things about me they were free to leave! There was naturally some banter.

However there was no presentation. The evening came and went. The only mention I received was in a letter read out on behalf of Catrin Edwards, the Chairman of the Welsh Conservatives, who was snowed in the Welsh hills. I would be dishonest if I did not admit to being hurt.

As Cheryl left (early) she ran into me.
"I hear you have a big job on in China" she said.

Nocturnal emotions

One of my guests for the evening was one of my best friends. Michael MacDougall is senior partner at Charles Stanley and Co in Milton Keynes and is my stockbroker. I had agreed to drive him back to his office (I do not drink so I am a popular chauffeur). Michael is an Old Harrovian.

We reached Milton Keynes around 1.00am and I parked my car at home in Leighton Buzzard thirty minutes later. Simon, my son-in-law, was staying as he had picked up some lecturing work in London. I hoped he was up because I was full of energy and wanted to discuss politics with him. A sleepy Judy crawled downstairs and told me that Simon was ill in bed with 'flu.

I turned the television on to watch the second cricket Test from Adelaide. England had taken three quick wickets but Australia were fighting back. But my mind was elsewhere.

I was cross with myself that I was angry with the Blue Dragons. I was well pleased with my chairmanship and several letters from Committee members seemed to justify that conclusion.

I blog weekly on www.enterprisebritain.com and I have been blunt about David Cameron, the Coalition Government, some other Conservatives, Downing Street advisers and Policy Exchange. It is read by some MPs and it crossed my mind that the Party had realised my stance. With the Conservatives you are either 'for us or against us'. If it is the latter you are out. Good public school rules.

I remembered what Nigel Horton, the English second row in the 1970s, once said. He was huge and had a distinguished international rugby career as well as leading the Birmingham side, Moseley. I played with him when I captained the North Midlands Colts against the Welsh. In the most appalling weather somewhere in South Wales we fought out a horrible match in mud. There was a ferocious fight and Horton went down. A Welsh forward had lashed out. I leant over Nigel and suggested revenge. He struggled to his feet and glowered at me.

I recalled what he had said when playing for Moseley against Swansea. He had been felled by a vicious kick.

"I give it, I take it" he said.

I looked at the wall in my study. I have collected photographs of many of the past Conservative leaders. I peered at Winston. "You changed sides" I thought.

As I slumbered one final question went through my head.

Was this 'sour grapes?' I had not made it politically to the level I would have wished. I was not rich. I was not 'inner circle'.

"Goodbye Dave" I said to myself and went to sleep.

II - Local Politics

My record as a local Conservative supporter is impressive!

I have never lost an MP!

From joining the South West Bedfordshire Conservative Association in the late 1980s to my decision to leave the Party in September 2010, I fought a number of general elections and always won (locally).

Sir David Madel was MP for the Constituency (which was varied by boundary changes from time to time) from 1983 to 2001. He was succeeded by Andrew Selous who remains the MP to the present day.

David Madel was hindered, with the benefit of hindsight, by his support for Edward Heath. He therefore struggled with Mrs Thatcher. He was fiercely pro-Europe. He was an outstanding constituency parliamentarian, scrupulously honest and with utter integrity. He was hugely respected both in South West Bedfordshire and in the House of Commons.

In the 1997 General Election, as Tony Blair swept to power, David Madel saw his share of the vote fall by 15.2% and he was re-elected by just 132 votes. The turnout was 75.8% as against 82% in 1992. I was in Singapore on business on the night of the election. The internet had yet to hit the communications sector and I telephoned Judy whilst having breakfast in the Shangri-la Hotel. As we connected David Mellor had just lost his seat.

Wise or not?

There was another candidate standing against David Madel in that campaign who achieved notoriety.

Tom Wise was a red-faced former policeman who had, within Leighton Buzzard where he lived, a reputation as a lover of good wines.

He stood against David Madel for the UK Independence Party attracting 446 votes which represented 0.8% of the total votes cast. He stood again in the General Election of 2001 against Andrew Selous. This time he polled 1,203 votes which was 2.74% of the overall total. He repeated the exercise in the General Election of 2005. His aggregate of 1,923 votes represented 4.2% of the total.

I knew Tom fairly well. He was large and loud. In 2002, at the age of 54, he was elected in the European Elections as a MEP for the UK Independence Party.

Over the following thirteen months he funded his love of wines (and fast cars) by channelling £39,000 into a secret bank account. He received from Brussels a monthly allowance of £3,000 for secretarial assistance. His 62 year old researcher, Lindsay Jenkins, received a small portion of this payment.

He was exposed in the Sunday newspapers and lost the UKIP whip but continued as an Independent MEP. He was sentenced in November 2009, in Southwark Crown Court, to two years in prison. He was not the first MEP to face jail. Ashley Mote, also a member of UKIP, was jailed in 2007 for benefit fraud.

During his trial the Prosecution Council said that if Tom Wise's fraud had remained undetected he could have accumulated £180,000. That would purchase quite a few bottles of Chateau Lafite.

Councillor Drury

The heart of the Conservative Party lies in its local Associations. Modern politics is seeing profound changes with postal voting, changes in voting systems, the use of the internet and tweeting, and the ever increasing power of the media. This was vividly demonstrated during the 2010 General Election campaign when the first of the Leaders' debates catapulted Nick Clegg, Leader of the Liberal Democrats, into greater public focus.

During the 1990s, as I became more involved in the activities of the South West Bedfordshire Conservative Association ("SWBCA"), local activity could and would have a significant influence on election results.

Whilst General Elections take place every four or five years, local campaigns were an annual event. We fought parish, town, district and county seats almost every year and before long European Parliamentary seats, on a regional basis, were being contested.

I spent many nights and weekends knocking on doors. It is not as difficult as one might imagine. Generally people were pleased to have the opportunity to debate issues with you although I seemed to spend most of my time listening! One evening, in a cul-de-sac in Plantation Ward (part of Leighton Buzzard), I rang the bell on three consecutive houses.

The first was answered by a practice nurse in one of the local surgeries: twenty minutes later I was in no doubt about what was needed in the NHS. The second was a senior school teacher, whose speciality in history seemed unconnected with the problems of young people, and the causation being their home environment. The last produced a local JP who left my ears ringing about the collapse of the judicial system.

I learnt the ropes quickly. Never campaign on a Friday evening. Most people are enjoying the first gin and tonic of the weekend, in front of the television, with a tray of food on their lap.

Having failed in my attempt to become a Parliamentary candidate I quickly teamed up with Andrew Selous, the chosen PPC, and the engine that was SWBCA went to work. I was selected to stand as the Conservative candidate in the County elections, being held at the same time, for Plantation Ward in Leighton Buzzard.

Andrew Selous is elected – just!

The 2001 General Election campaign was delayed by the rampant outbreak of foot-and-mouth disease which devastated much of rural Britain. It took place on Thursday 7 June 2001. Tony Blair won a second term with a massive majority of 167 seats (12 down on 1997) on the low turnout of 59.4% compared to 71.4% in 1997. William Hague struggled to make any impact, resigned and handed over to Iain Duncan Smith.

In South West Bedfordshire Andrew Selous worked himself into the ground. He is around six foot, seven inches tall, articulate, experienced, and Christian in his outlook. From the day he was elected he has made a remarkable impact on our communities. He fights causes. He will play politics, if he has to do so, but what he really wants to do is to change people's lives for the better.

In 2006 he was appointed a Shadow Work and Pensions Minister. However, much to my disappointment, he did not gain a cabinet position, becoming Parliamentary Private Secretary to Iain Duncan Smith, who was Secretary of State for Work and Pensions.

The count at Dunstable Leisure Centre, on the night of 7 June 2001, was eventful. Andrew

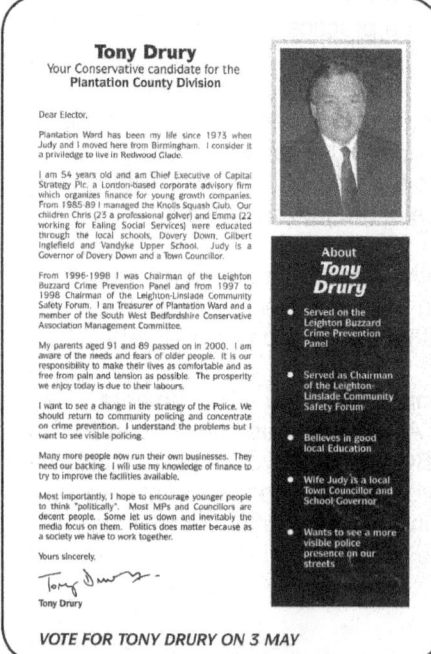

The County Council Elections actually took place on 7 June 2001

Date, the Labour candidate fought a good campaign. With the continuing popularity of Tony Blair, and the marginality of the seat, it was tense, very tense. Tom Wise was standing for UKIP and was striding around in his Falstaff manner. I cannot remember the Liberal Democrat who was to take nearly 15% of the vote.

The Leisure Centre was big and there were many tables. Hours pass and one wondered what is happening. Around midnight there was a meeting between the Returning Officer and the candidates' agents. There was a recount.

Sir Neville Bowman-Shaw, our President, appeared with six bottles of champagne. He and I drank two of them before the evening ended.

There was a second recount. Then a rumour circulated. Somebody had found a bundle of 500 votes and they were for Andrew Selous. Around three in the morning Andrew Selous was elected. He gave a great speech and Andrew Date didn't. Sir Neville was magnificent and inspirational. Andrew was exhausted. Everybody hugged everybody.

Judy and I dashed home, grabbed some sleep and rushed back, early on Friday morning, to the Leisure Centre for the County Council elections. The initial bundling of the votes suggested I had lost. One of the local councillors (a Conservative), who did not like me, came up to my side: "You've lost Drury" he trilled.

I won and gave an impromptu speech because I had never realised I had to say something. We had a party at our home that night. It really is good to win elections.

Reflections

I was well known in the Plantation Ward mainly because during the 1980s I had co-owned the Knolls Squash Club. This was housed in 'The Knolls' a country house that was, originally, the home of the Barrett family, one of founding parties of Barclays

Bank. We turned this into a hotel and sold out in 1988. It became, and still is, an old people's home.

County Councillor Drury

I was a County Councillor for nearly three years. I relished the work, every meeting, all the bouts with the Liberal Democrats, the frustrations of dealing with County Officials and almost being sacked.

I was a member of the Community and Environment Committee. The Chairman was Councillor Peter Roberts, husband of the fearsome Councillor Angela Roberts, Leader of the County Council.

The day before Committee I had realised that the bridge over the Grand Union Canal was to be closed for repairs. The alternative route into Leighton Buzzard, down Heath Road, was also closed for repairs to the pavements. The western route into Linslade was also being repaired. I realised that Leighton Buzzard was about to be cut off.

After getting up at 4.00am I prepared coloured maps for all the members of the Committee.

The Chairman started the meeting at 9.30am and I raised a point of order. In fairness to Councillor Roberts he handled the ensuing events skilfully. I was on a mission. He said I had to adhere to the agenda. I distributed my maps. He said it was not the role of the Committee to consider these operational matters. I said I had I been elected a County Councillor to serve the community.

Help came from an unexpected quarter. The Labour Councillor realised that his ward would also be isolated. Within minutes the Chairman was 'surrounded'. He called for the Council Director. That night the bridge was re-opened.

As we left the meeting Councillor Roberts came up to me: "Don't you ever do that again" he snarled.

The "Leighton Buzzard on Sunday": 1 February 2004

Resignation

With the benefit of hindsight, and perhaps if I had given up alcohol a little earlier (see Chapter Five), I would have assessed my situation at the County Council differently. I was right to hurry back to St. Helen's Capital and take the action needed to strengthen the executive team. However, I realised that I should have given the leader, Councillor Angela Roberts, time to find a way forward.

Oak Bank School

My three years as a County Councillor were some of the happiest I have ever experienced.

As part of my responsibilities I became Chair of Governors at Oak Bank School. This is an EBD centre. The acronym stands for 'Emotional and Behavioural Difficulties'.

Bedfordshire is a small county and, at that time, chose to place all those pupils needing special teaching (a number were seriously socially troubled children) in one school. This produced its own challenges.

The pupils were transported by taxis because they were not able to travel on public services. Some would be collected from home (sometimes 'their' home but, on occasions, from County centres) as early as seven o'clock in the morning. Many were on prescriptive drug regimes and the teachers were faced with the responsibility of ensuring each child was receiving the required dosage.

The school had staffing (albeit not budget) problems and violence was breaking out. I was lucky enough to have a superb Governing Body and established great working relationships with the County education executives. The processes frustrated me but you never better the system. I had a focus and together we ensured the future of Oak Bank School. The current Head Teacher had already established himself as a professional of outstanding ability and I knew that I just had to achieve the stability to allow him to lead.

The visit of Ofsted will stay long in the memory. I have grave misgivings on the validity of the Ofsted process. I am all for accountability but the regime of fear that swept the country, sometimes fuelled by individuals who, in a number of cases, were failed teachers in their own right, is not, in my opinion, the optimum regulatory route.

To be fair Oak Bank represented a massive challenge and tested all of us. What mattered to me was the fate of the fifty children for whom we were responsible. Yet, when I was faced with a teacher, who had just been attacked and injured, it became hard to keep that focus in place.

The Man who lay on the Carpet

For some of the procedures, as Chair of Governors, I was the last cog in the Appeals wheel. When I was told of my first case I read the file and thought about it carefully. I spoke to the County Officer and asked if I could conduct the interview in the pupil's own home. I reasoned that with me wearing a business suit, sitting in Oak Bank School, the parents might struggle to relax. County agreed and off I went towards Bedford.

I stepped over the broken bike and uncollected refuse sacks and knocked on the front door. From the start his mother hardly stopped talking throughout the whole evening. She brought out file after file which she had maintained about her son. We went through the whole history, appeal after appeal.

The father (I think he was the other parent) was huge. During the time I was in their house he lay on the carpet smoking something that had a rather strange odour. The visit ended with me being shown into the son's bedroom to see his collection of reptiles. The black hissing viper, from West Africa, took an instant dislike to me.

I drove home a bit depressed. I was out of my depth. Hours were spent going over the whole evening. I wrote a report and raised my concerns about the boy to the County officials.

A few weeks later Oak Bank School held a Parents' evening. After an hour the Head Teacher came up to me. "Have you seen?" he exclaimed. "What?" I asked. The parents, for the first time, had turned up. The man (possibly the father) came up and crushed my hand. I checked quickly to ascertain whether he had brought the viper with him.

In my heart of hearts, I know that I departed Bedford County in the wrong way. It was the nearest I ever came to real politics and I loved every single minute.

III - Change of Leader: Iain Duncan Smith and Michael Howard

Iain Duncan Smith, ("IDS"), was born in Edinburgh, Scotland in 1954. In 1982 he married Elizabeth Fremantle, the daughter of the 5th Baron Cottesloe. In 1992 he became the Conservative Member of Parliament for Chingford and Woodford Green in succession to Norman Tebbit.

From June 1997 to June 1999 he was Shadow Secretary of State for Social Security. He moved to Defence until 13 September 2001 when he replaced William Hague as Leader of the Conservative Party. He defeated Kenneth Clarke in the final round, the latter losing votes because of his staunch pro-European stance and a public vote of support by Lady Thatcher for IDS.

Whatever the personal merits are, and were, of IDS, as Leader he was simply dire.

In fairness the Conservative Party were still, amazingly, in denial about Tony Blair and simply failed to realise why Middle England had deserted the Conservative ship.

The real problem was that IDS had no media skills and little, if any, impact. On one occasion, our four local Conservative Associations united for an IDS dinner at Woburn. We were standing in a pre-dinner circle when one of the wives asked when the Leader was joining us. IDS was standing two positions away from her.

At the 2002 Conservative Conference he spoke the memorable words; "the quiet man is here to stay, and he's turning up the volume." In November 2002 he was under more pressure. He stated to the Party: "My message is simple and stark, unite or die."

Political Associations are loyal to their leaders. You have to believe in election victory which is why you go out, night after night, and knock on doors.

Whilst attending the Conservative Spring conference in Harrogate in 2001, I was gaining great confidence in William Hague, who was creating a real impact with Ffion at his side.

I found myself late at night at a bar with a broadsheet journalist. I gave him my best Party speech about the coming victory. He took about four minutes of my rhetoric. He turned to me, quietly put his half empty beer glass on the bar, and said: "You are a f*****g idiot."

Letter to 'The Times': Thursday 7 November 2002

The problem was that he was right.

I retained the same naive conviction in IDS and, as shown in the letter to 'The Times' above, was fighting his corner. I did, however, gain some credibility when I wrote:

"If, in (say) 12 months' time, either Iain Duncan Smith himself or a significant number of MPs have genuine doubts, there is a correct procedure to follow. This present skirmish is not the way."

Within months of the letter being published IDS was fighting for his political life.

A Coffee with Sir David Madel

At an October meeting of the South West Bedfordshire Councillors, chaired by Councillor Angela Roberts, and held on a Saturday morning in a Dunstable school, there was a spontaneous outburst of frustration over IDS. Andrew Selous handled the comments with great tact. What amazed me was that nobody could think of a possible replacement. The only person mentioned in that respect was William Hague!

On 15 October 2003 IDS wrote to all Conservative MPs. He included an increasingly desperate paragraph:

"My wife and I have this week been the subject of an unfounded and deeply offensive smear campaign, designed to discredit not just myself but the whole Party. I intend to rebut these allegations with all my power, so that our Party can again focus on the things which matter to the people of Britain."

On Wednesday 22 October 2003 I received at telephone call at my London office from Sir David Madel. He would be arriving at Liverpool Street Station within thirty minutes. Would I like to meet him for a cup of coffee?

When we settled down, in a restaurant in London Wall, David said that he was on his way to the Carlton Club in Mayfair for a meeting of the Paddocks. This was a group of former Members of Parliament who had been put out to grass.

We mulled over a few local matters and then I related to Sir David the events of the meeting of Bedfordshire Councillors.

Sir David looked at me.

"Michael Howard will be the next leader" he said quietly.

Media momentum

'The Times' phoned me on Thursday 23 October 2003. As an Association Chairman I was used to receiving press calls although usually the objective was to try to gain a viewpoint from a cross section of people within the Conservative Party.

On this occasion, knowing what I had been told and believed, I was more forceful in my response to the questions about the future of IDS. Around 8.00pm I received a call from a sub-editor who said they were going to quote me. He read out the copy and I agreed.

The headlines in 'The Times' the next morning were; "Clarke to throw his hat in the ring" and the front page article included my quote:

"Tony Drury, chairman in the Bedfordshire South West constituency said: "It has become absolutely inevitable for IDS to stand for reselection. It is the only way to clear the air. I would personally like him to stay, but he has made mistakes. The situation is very serious. I would say he has a 50-50 chance of being re-selected."

The reason I phrased my opinion in this way was that I tried to reflect the overall attitudes I had heard at the meeting of the Councillors and I wanted to support Andrew Selous. He had been a keen supporter of IDS and I was aware that he was finding the situation difficult.

From that moment my phone did not stop and I completed a number of radio interviews. Sky News broadcast live from our house on the following Sunday and the BBC included an interview in its news programmes.

One call I received was from a glamorous sounding TV executive who worked for Andrew Neil. He, at that time, had a mid-morning TV show. They were keen I should appear. My problem was that I had a Board Meeting of St. Helen's Capital the next day. She was rather effective in persuading me.

We agreed I would telephone the Board members and, if they approved (which they did), I would come. I was to phone her at 8.00am the next morning.

When I spoke to her she was rather apologetic but said that I would not be needed.

As I arrived home that evening Judy told me that she had watched the Andrew Neil show and that his guest was Peter Stringfellow. Apparently they had been joking on air that Andrew had been to Stringfellows the previous evening and had such a good time with the owner that he had invited him on to his show. Well, I mused, not a bad person by whom to be gazumped!

On Friday 24 October 2003 the headline in 'The Evening Standard' was *"Is IDS all out: Donors are deserting, MPs are gathering signatures against him and even his own whips are talking him down. The next few days will decide the Tory's leader's fate."*

On Tuesday 28 October 2003 25 MPs forced a vote of confidence which took place the next day. IDS said that he welcomed the chance to end: *"this ludicrous leadership speculation."*

IDS lost the vote of confidence by 90 votes to 75.

Eight days later, on 6 November 2003, he stepped down as Leader when Michael Howard was elected unopposed. The most serious alternative, David Davis, had withdrawn from any possible election citing Party unity.

IDS seemed to lose it at this point. On 1 November 2003 he was quoted as saying "I told the 1922 Committee on Wednesday: Anyone who wants this job needs their head examining."

He also said: *"I'm a writer now and I'll be with my family. I intend to make the most of it."*

Less than two weeks after his resignation his novel 'The Devil's Time' was published. It received poor reviews and was never produced in paperback.

In 2004 IDS formed the Centre for Social Justice, a centre-right think tank which sought to find innovative policies for tackling poverty.

On 12 May 2010 he became Secretary of State for Work and Pensions in the Coalition Government.

Michael Howard

The new leader of the Conservative Party had baggage. In particular a well-remembered interview with Jeremy Paxman and a barbed, and oft repeated, comment, from Ann Widdecombe, that he had "something of the night" about him.

Michael Howard fought a resolute and disciplined General Election Campaign in 2005. He employed an Australian strategist, Lynton Crosby, who had worked successfully for the oft re-elected John Howard.

I attended a breakfast meeting at Conservative Campaign Headquarters in Westminster. The office staff were treating Lynton Crosby like a god.

"Lynton will be here in seven minutes" they announced.

"Lynton is nearer now" they continued.

After thirty minutes of the much delayed breakfast I was struggling with Lynton Crosby. Was I the only person present who realised that he had never fought a three main Party election?

Wow, was he impressed with himself! The breakfast guests were the cream of the Party and I was on my best behaviour.

My turn came and I asked Lynton about the overall campaign strategy and suggested that, despite his wonderful theories on marginal seats, the economy would play a big part in voters' opinions.

Lynton Crosby told me that "the voters are tired of the economy." Those were his exact words.

He later was to be involved in the disgraceful removal of Howard Flight as a MP (as told in Chapter Four), an event which also involved Andrew Mackay MP, who features later.

Michael Howard lost the election and immediately resigned. We were, however, to meet again in 2010 as explained below.

Lord Howard of Lympne

Having handed over to David Cameron as Leader of the Conservative Party, Michael Howard settled down in the House of Commons as a backbench Member of Parliament.

In the 2005 General Election he retained his seat of Folkestone and Hythe with a 8.9% swing in his favour. He polled 26,161 votes which was 53.9% of the total. He occasionally made headlines with his comments on law and order but it was as one member of a married couple that he gained more publicity.

The other party was Sandra Howard, formerly a model, and now on her way to becoming a bestselling novelist. In 2010, when Michael Howard was to re-enter my life, the paperback version of her third book, 'A Matter of Loyalty', was issued.

This marvellous story was a modern day political thriller set in England and involved bombs in the West End of London, a harassed Home Secretary, a young Muslim newspaper reporter, a love affair and a good ending.

'The Mail on Sunday', in its edition of 14 February 2010, published a three page profile of Michael and Sandra Howard (she is also a travel writer) on holiday in Peloponnese in Greece.

A few months later events were to bring Michael Howard and myself together. The Blue Dragon Club had lost its President Lord Walker. It was decided to ask Welsh born Michael Howard to consider succeeding him. My friend Andrew Mackay agreed to arrange a social meeting for the three of us.

Lunch at Wiltons

This took place in early September at Wiltons. Andrew Mackay arrived first and then Michael Howard joined us. For the first few minutes they engaged in eager conversation and I thought that Andrew was slipping in to his Public Relations role (see Chapter Six) with ease. They then noticed that I was sitting there.

Michael Howard was relishing his peerage and was in high spirits. I am not sure whether he was serious but he implied that he had little intention of playing a major part in the House of Lords. His wife was a travel writer and they were going to have lots of holidays. He said that he did not really want to be President of the Blue Dragon Club but that as I was buying him a nice lunch at Wiltons he would agree providing he did not have to do very much. He reasoned that, as Sandra was likely to be organising frequent foreign trips, he could not commit to anything.

I said that was not good enough. We had a discussion and we reached an agreement that if he could set the date for the annual dinner (he had already said he could not attend the 2010 event) he would guarantee to be present.

On 20 September 2010 I contacted Michael to explain that I was leaving the Conservative Party and my reasons for this decision. He replied that he "strongly disagreed" with my criticisms of David Cameron but acknowledged that I was entitled to my opinions.

Michael Howard did not become President of the Blue Dragon Club. Lord Walker was succeeded by Lord Howe of Aberavon.

IV - Lord Lamont and Lord Flight

Lord Lamont of Lerwick

The Right Honourable the Lord Lamont of Lerwick is an important historical and political character. Norman Lamont was the Conservative Member of Parliament for Kingston-upon-Thames from May 1972 until 1 May 1997. He was Chancellor of the Exchequer from 28 November 1990 until 27 May 1993 when he was 'sacked' by John Major. This period was dominated by the decision for the UK to leave the European Exchange Rate Mechanism ("ERM").

On Wednesday 15 June 2005, at around 2.15pm, Lord Lamont stopped speaking to me. He has not spoken to me since. He has cold shouldered me on five different occasions.

During 2003 – 2004 I had met and begun to enjoy the company of Norman Lamont. After one particularly pleasant lunch he sent me a copy of his autobiography which he personally signed.

'In Office' by Norman Lamont

This proved to be one of the best 'political' books I have read and is a 'must' for all students of political history. It was published by Warner Books in 1999.

A clue to its effectiveness is to be found in the 'Introduction':

"This book is not an autobiography. It is merely an account of my time at the Treasury....I have never found autobiographies with accounts of how people went to school with no shoes or how they and all their contemporaries were a brilliant generation at university very gripping."

Inevitably Chapter 9: 'Black or White Wednesday?' will attract the most attention as Lord Lamont details the agonies of the UK's exit from the ERM. This took place on 16 September 1992. The then Chancellor is not quick to criticise but his frustration with John

Major shows up at times: *"He seemed unwilling to face up to the issue."*

There is a passage which caused me to gulp. He is

"*The Evening Standard*" 11 March 2005

telling of the post-ERM events:

"I was anxious to get down to Canterbury to see James and Sophie, so we set off, with Rosemary driving. When we arrived outside the school gates of my son's school house we put the car into a parking bay and got out. A small boy, not more than six or seven, holding his mother's hand, pointed to me and said, 'Mum, it's that man who has ruined the country.' I shall never forget that moment."

'In Office' is, however, much, much more as the reader is taken through the Conservative leadership election of 1990, the economic problems, the ERM and the UK's exit, the seeds of recovery and Norman Lamont's resignation. Chapter 22: 'The Major Years, 1990-97' is particularly interesting.

In a paper titled 'Whatever happened to the Golden Legacy: the economic background to the 2005 Budget', written by Ruth Lea, Director of the Centre for Policy Studies, it was stated that:

"Gordon Brown's fiscal reforms were not revolutionary. They merely consolidated the Lamont reforms which had succeeded in reducing inflation and delivering sustainable growth".

I was to unite Norman Lamont and Ruth Lea a few weeks later but with an outcome I could never have anticipated.

The St. Helen's Capital lunch

In the spring of 2005 I was feeling more confident about the prospects for St. Helen's Capital. There was a stable Government and the Chancellor of the Exchequer was at the peak of his powers. The Aim and PLUS-quoted markets were in a Bull phase. I went for growth.

I decided to start a monthly lunch for key customers and pencilled in Wednesday 15 June 2005 for the first of these occasions. I wrote to Norman Lamont and asked if he would be our guest of honour. He replied and confirmed that he would. I asked Ruth Lea if she would join us and, again, I received an affirmative answer.

Mark and I agreed a guest list. We booked Gow's in Old Broad Street near to Liverpool Street Station. It is a world class fish restaurant.

The day of the lunch arrived and by 12.45pm we were sitting in the restaurant awaiting the arrival of our guest of honour. I

15 June 2005 at Gow's Restaurant. Norman Lamont is fourth from the left. I am opposite and Ruth Lea is second from the right. On the right-hand side is Mark Warde-Norbury.

chatted to Ruth Lea and asked her if her publication was receiving further praise. She seemed pleased to respond.

Norman Lamont arrived. Heads turned. He was a little irritable and he asked that we order the food straight away. The Chablis seemed to help.

The service at Gow's is efficient and slowly Norman thawed. I asked him an economics question and one of the guests disputed his answer. We were away. Norman Lamont on form is formidable and after an hour I was beginning to relax. I knew my Finance Director would make a fuss about the bill. I was in my comfort zone. This was St. Helen's Capital joining the London financial community.

Towards the end of the lunch I made a weak joke about having to pay the bill and so did anybody mind if I did a PR bit! Most of the attendees were clients and were used to my poor humour. I 'sold' St. Helen's and noticed that Norman Lamont was nodding. As importantly our clients seemed to be enjoying the occasion..

A sudden end

However, a few minutes after my speech, an incident took place which disturbed our guest of honour.

Within a few minutes Norman Lamont had left the table, without a further word being spoken. He was closely followed by Ruth Lea. I chased after them but I knew the damage was done.

I wrote to Norman and I wrote again. Neither he, nor Ruth Lea, chose to communicate with me.

I have, since that lunch, met Norman Lamont on possibly five or six 'Conservative' occasions including one at Howard Flight's 1,900 Club. Lord Lamont has continued to ignore me.

We built St. Helen's Capital into a successful corporate finance house, in part, by developing some wonderful relationships. Norman Lamont was, until that day, the one I valued the most. He is a fascinating and highly intelligent man with the ability to laugh at himself. I never lost a sense of privilege when I met and dined with him. He is one of the great financial figures of the last fifty years.

The canons of financial investment are 'pain' (you lose some money) and 'gain' (it's a winner). Norman Lamont took me through those emotions and I was pretty fed-up with the way it ended. But it was worth it.

Lord Flight

In the world of small-cap companies in which I work Howard Flight is a giant. He is hugely respected both for his personal, and financial success at Guinness Flight and for his contribution to City life. He is Chairman of the Enterprise Investment Scheme Association ("EISA") and works hard for its members. He has also promoted 'The Conservative City Circle' which brings together the City (usually on a Monday evening) and senior Conservative Politicians.

During the latter part of the new decade, and following Michael Howard's Election defeat, I was occasionally telephoned by Conservative Campaign Headquarters to ask if I was attending such-and-such event. Following the victory of David Cameron, attendances at 'City Circle' soared with perhaps fifteen hundred or more youthful executives wanting to hear and meet David himself and others such as George Osborne.

THE CONSERVATIVE CITY CIRCLE
INVITES YOU TO A RECEPTION WITH
GEORGE OSBORNE, MP
SHADOW CHANCELLOR OF THE EXCHEQUER
ON
MONDAY, 11TH MAY 2009
AT
THE GRANGE CITY HOTEL, 8-10 COOPERS ROW, LONDON EC3N 2BQ
HOSTED BY THE GRANGE CITY HOTEL
Conservative City Circle

City Circle event Monday 11 May 2009

I first met Howard in 2004 and by early 2005 we were corresponding on political and Treasury issues. Howard was interested in my building up of St. Helen' Capital although, at that time, I was not to realise the significant events which were to take place at a later date.

Political catastrophe

Howard Flight was MP for Arundel and South Downs from 1 May 1997 to 5 May 2005. He held several Shadow Cabinet posts including Shadow Chief Secretary to the Treasury.

The incident, however, that was to completely baffle me, took place on 24 March 2005. On that day Howard resigned as deputy Chairman of the Conservative Party. The reasons include a ludicrous decision by Michael Howard.

During the 2005 General Election campaign Howard Flight made comments at a Conservative Way Forward meeting which, unbeknown to him, was being secretly recorded. Flight argued for deeper spending cuts than were being promoted in the Manifesto. However, a blind German student, Joerg Tretow, who was Chairman of Labour Students at London's Queen Mary College, tape recorded Flight's presentation, and passed it to Labour sources, who gave it to 'The Times'.

The Conservative leader Michael Howard withdrew the party whip. He then announced that Flight was no longer an approved candidate and thus he could not contest the General Election for his consistency. Both Flight and the local officials initially resisted, but Arundel and South Downs, having had a visit from Andrew Mackay, caved in. Nick Herbert was approved and subsequently won the seat for the Conservatives. The newspapers enjoyed the whole event.

'The Daily Telegraph':26 March 2005, quoting John Reid, the Labour Health Secretary, who said that *"[Howard Flight] has revealed in private what the Tories dare not admit in public – that they are secretly planning cuts to public services over and above the £35 billion they have already confirmed."*

It is interesting to wonder whether in 2010 David Cameron lost an election he should have won because he displayed the same timidity and then told Britain it was bankrupt.

I was in regular contact with Howard Flight and we had lunch at Gow's when he was clearly a distressed person. He was later to write to me, on 24 April 2005, as follows:

"I reached the conclusion that I could not run as an independent for several reasons. The polls are neck and neck, and I genuinely want to see the Conservative Party win which the high profile of standing as an independent could damage....I have also tried to conduct myself in a principled fashion..."

I knew that Campaign Headquarters were concerned about Howard's tendency to speak outside the Party mandate and he did have a reputation for controversial rhetoric. However the decision to, effectively, sack him concerned me in three ways:

1. It drove a coach and horses through the Party Rule Book.
2. It ignored the 'rights' of the local party.
3. It lost Parliament an outstanding MP.

Howard returned to the City but, before long, he was talking about the advice he was offering to David Cameron.

The Globalisation Institute

David Cameron giving his speech: 6 November 2006

In March 2006 Howard wrote to me and invited me to become involved with The Globalisation Institute where he was Chairman. He described it as a 'Think Tank' set up and headed by Alex Singleton.

Alex had previously been Research Director at the Adam Smith Institute. I read several of their publications: 'Green and Pleasant Land (advocating radical reform to the Common Agricultural Policy), 'Trade

Justice or Free Trade?' and 'WTO2005 and Beyond'.
I built up a healthy respect for Alex Singleton who was bright, hard working and focused. We were to work well together and on 6 November 2006 St. Helen's Capital sponsored an event for the Institute at the Leathersellers' Hall. David Cameron came and made a terrific impact including delivering a well thought through speech.

It proved difficult to fund the Institute. Generally people felt that Globalisation is a merited objective as long as they are not asked to finance it!

Alex came to see me and told of an opportunity that had arisen at 'The Daily Telegraph' to blog for their website. Although I was pleased for him my inner concerns came true. Before long his talents were further recognised and he became full time journalist.

He closed down the operations of the Institute and organised its safe transfer to another body. As this publication was being completed Alex left the 'Telegraph' and set up his own business.

The 1900 Club

On 13 June 2008 Howard wrote to me and invited me to join The 1900 Club. He had recently taken over as Chairman.

The Club was formed in 1906 by a number of Unionists who were about to retire from the House of Commons. They were *"desirous of preserving ties of friendships formed with many of their fellow members.....resolved to form a Club, to be called 'The 1900 Club', to meet and dine together periodically."*

I was to enjoy some marvellous evenings at The Carlton Club, at Boodle's (The Harrovian Club), at Brooks's (Robert Harvey's Club) and St Stephen's Club. We listened to speakers including Eric Pickles, Iain Duncan Smith, Damien Green, Simon Heffer and Sir Paul Stevenson. On occasions we linked up with the Centre of Policy Studies. On one occasion the speaker was Lord Lamont. He did not speak to me.

I felt I had no choice but to leave the Club in late 2010 as I was no longer a Conservative member.

St. Helen's Capital

My relationship with Howard continued and before leaving St. Helen's in 2006 I discussed with him whether he would consider joining the Board as a non-executive Director. This happened and my understanding is that he and the other directors formed a united group.

A new Executive Team was recruited from Daniel Stewart Securities. Before long the company was struggling from one problem to the next. During the summer of 2008 I telephoned Howard and suggested that the Board's only hope of recovering from the issues they were facing was to invite me back to sort it out.

Howard hesitated but said that he wanted to give the executive directors a final chance. I wondered whether to tell him that I had met two of his executives in St. Helen's Place following what might have been an enjoyable lunch.

On 27 May 2009 I wrote to Howard and presented him with a business opportunity which, in my opinion, might be in the best interests of the St. Helen's Capital shareholders. My file note of 3 June 2009 read as follows:

"It is an open secret in the market place that SHC are in deep trouble and looking for a deal.

On Monday 1 June 2009 I met with Howard Flight. He was not particularly interested in SHC (he was working out whether he could get back into Parliament via Julie Kirkbride's seat in Bromsgrove). We had an utterly confusing conversation about my letter....

Howard told me that Mark Warde-Norbury the Chairman of SHC had been told by the non-executives to sort matters out and I should see him.

Mark was candid about matters and we had a chat about my proposal. He said he would come back to me."

Neither he, nor Howard, ever did.

St. Helen's business was eventually sold to a securities house and the shell was reborn as a new corporate finance business. Several shareholders stayed in touch with me and regularly expressed their disappointment in the loss in value of their shares.

Lord Flight

In November 2010 Howard Flight was proposed for a peerage. Within days he hit the headlines by suggesting that welfare cuts would encourage the poor to have more children as the number of middle-class children decline.

This was a week after Lord Young of Grantham, David Cameron's Business Adviser, was sacked for saying that many people had *"never had it so good."*

Lord Lamont and Lord Flight were two major influences on me during my period of involvement with the Conservative Party.

V - The Blue Dragon Club

In Chapter One I explained the circumstances which took place at the 2010 Annual Dinner of the Blue Dragon Club. What follows is a brief background to that event.

The link to my involvement with the Welsh Conservatives goes back to November 2005 when my wife and I were invited to the annual dinner of the Montgomeryshire Conservative Party at Welshpool by my friend Robert Harvey whom I had first met in London.

Robert, a former columnist for 'The Daily Telegraph' and an assistant editor for 'The Economist', is a distinguished author. His special subject is current affairs. 'The Return of the Strong: The Drift to Global Disorder' is perhaps one of his best books. But, as he once told me, he writes on politics and international matters because they are his first love, and on history, "because that is what pays the bills". 'American Shogun: MacArthur, Hirohito and the American Duel with Japan' gained the following recommendation from the 'Sunday Telegraph':

"Harvey wields his pen like a sabre, slashing with gusto at cant and received wisdom, as he leads an exhilarating charge into history."

My own favourite from his many works is 'The War of Wars: the epic struggle between Britain and France 1793-1815.' His Napoleonic narrative covering the twenty-two year struggle between the two greatest powers in Europe is 800 pages of well told history.

Robert lives in Meifod in Powys, a few miles north-east of Welshpool. He was the Conservative Member of Parliament for Clwyd South-West from 1983 – 1987. Robert is a member of Brooks's Club in St. James Street, Piccadilly and we continue to meet there on a regular basis. He is a passionate thinker about Conservative politics and has the intellectual ability to explain to me complex economic and social issues.

At the Montgomeryshire Dinner I met Simon Baynes, a merchant banker from London. Earlier in the year Simon had stood in the General Election as the Conservative candidate for Montgomeryshire. He came second to Lembit Opik, the Liberal Democrat , who had held the seat since 1997.

My association with Simon, who is now Deputy Chairman of the Welsh Conservatives and a County Councillor for Powys, flourished. He is an amazingly self-driven individual who has tried hard to find another seat to fight. He invited me to the Blue Dragon Dinner in London in 2007 and shortly afterwards, asked me if I would chair the new Blue Dragon Club.

The idea was to link the political work of the Welsh Conservatives with supporters in London and elsewhere outside Wales. At the heart of the matter was a wish to raise funds to help the electioneering process.

The Welsh Conservatives had virtually been wiped out in 1997 as a huge reaction to Mrs. Thatcher set in. By 2005 there were three Welsh Conservatives in Westminster. In the new Welsh Assembly the Conservatives were struggling to gain influence. Under Nick Bourne they began to get stronger and had an outstanding result in the European elections of 2008.

The Blue Dragon Committee

Simon Baynes introduced me to Lord Peter Walker who agreed to be our President and slowly the work, during 2008 and 2009, of the Blue Dragon Club developed. The Committee evolved into what, for me, was perhaps the most committed and talented group of people I had ever met.

From Wales there was Catrin Edwards, Chairman of the Welsh Conservatives, and Lyndon Johnson, their President. Jeff James was the Vice Chairman, Finance. Caroline Oag, a vivacious and utterly talented woman was Communications Officer (and developed an excellent website) and Sarah Timothy was Youth Officer.

It was Sarah who, at one of our early meeting, set the juices flowing with a brilliant presentation on her proposals for engaging the young people of Wales in politics.

Simon Mort, who was to take over from me as Acting Chairman, and who became Events Officer, was one of those Conservatives who, if asked to run through a brick wall for the Party, would suggest that he run through two brick walls.

Dr. Paul Stafford, who was Fund-raising Officer, started slowly but later demonstrated his Queen's Counsel skills in his distillation of an issue. I remember saying, after he had finished, that next time I was in front of a judge, could he be on my side.

Richard Hopkin, who wants to be an MP, became a friend. When I visited his flat in Clerkenwell he preceded our discussion with a recital of Chopin music which he played beautifully on his expensive piano.

Havard Hughes, Evan Price and Bernard Gentry were all contributive members of the Committee. Bernard was a hard working Association member who built up to expressing his point of view. When he did he was decidedly centre of the Party. I used to privately agree with everything he said but always maintained my Chairman's impartiality: "Er...thank you Bernard...must move on..er..full agenda today."

The Administrator was Sally Dyson who was simply a lovely person. She was modestly efficient and committed. We 'gelled' almost immediately and the acclaimed success of the Blue Dragon Club was down to her and to Simon Baynes who really acted as my mentor.

When I made mistakes Simon helped me. He was unfailingly encouraging. Whenever I spoke at Blue Dragon events I always acknowledged the part that Simon had played in the formation of the Club and its success.

The Club's objectives

If I achieved anything at the Blue Dragon Club, it was to keep the process on a focused basis. I had spent too many wasted political hours engaged in self-interested debates on topics which led nowhere.

Early on the Committee spent some considerable time discussing and agreeing a set of objectives which were to hold us together. They were:

1. To represent people based outside Wales who have their heart in Wales with the objective of achieving Conservative election success in Wales
2. To raise campaign funds for the Welsh Conservative Party.
3. To provide a convivial meeting place for Welsh Conservative supporters.
4. To provide practical support and expertise for campaigning in Wales.
5. To encourage young people to become involved with the Welsh Conservative Party.

At our early meetings (usually in London although at a later stage we decided to alternate with Cardiff) I would read out the objectives and Sally always printed them at the top of the Minutes.

Cheryl Gillan

The Right Honourable Cheryl Gillan MP is Secretary of State for Wales and has represented Chesham and Amersham (a very safe Conservative seat) since 1992. She is close to David Cameron who has been actively supportive of the political process in Wales. They both knew that to win the 2010 General Election, Wales needed to increase its representation from three Members of Parliament to eleven or twelve. After the success in the European election in 2008 the target was thirteen or even more.

The eventual result was eight.

Until my difficulties with Cheryl in September 2010, as described in Chapter One, I thought I was 'close' to her in that we had regular lunches and met at various events. In particular we both attended 'Wales in London' occasions which were (and are) organised by the marvellous Robert John.

Prior to the 2010 General Election Robert John held four dinners at which each of the political parties presented their policies. The winners, by my judgement, were the Liberal Democrats. Nick Clegg came and went but the star was Kirstie Williams. She was feisty and she cared.

Plaid Cymru simply had no real political message and the fact they only won three seats in the 2010 General Election came as no surprise.

Cheryl and Nick Bourne represented the Conservatives and did well. For Labour the new leader Carwen James and Peter Hain appeared. I was sitting with Cheryl that evening and she was subjected to the usual Hain treatment. It was politics at its rough-house worst.

Cheryl was committed to, and supportive of, the Blue Dragon Club. She attended virtually all our events and usually spoke effectively and with passion. Being Welsh - she was born in Llandaff, Cardiff - this was real.

BLUE DRAGON CLUB

The President, Officers and Committee invite you to
THE BLUE DRAGON CLUB ANNUAL DINNER
Guest Speaker
The Right Hon The Lord Hunt of Wirral M.B.E.
Former Secretary of State for Wales

On Wednesday, 11th November 2009
7.00pm for 7.30pm
at The Army & Navy Club, 36 Pall Mall, London SW1Y 5JN

Black Tie
Tickets £80 inc. pre-dinner drinks
RSVP: Sally Dyson - email: admin@bluedragonclub.net, phone: 0207 976 5785
If you are unable to attend but would like to make a donation, please see the enclosed application form.
www.bluedragonclub.net

The 2009 Dinner

The Blue Dragon Dinner: Wednesday 11 November 2009

The Club seemed to go from strength to strength and perhaps peaked at the 2009 Annual Dinner. This was held at The Army and Navy Club, in Pall Mall.

The former Secretary of State for Wales, The Lord Hunt of Wirral MBE and Cheryl were the speakers. Simon Mort raised substantial funds with a virtuoso performance as the auctioneer. There was, of course, the inevitable raffle.

I pulled out all the stops for this occasion and invited thirty guests from 'the City'. I gave a robust speech to end the evening imploring everyone to support the Welsh political effort and pointing out to the various politicians present that my guests, from the small-cap sector of the London financial markets, represented an important part of the London community. My pals liked that.

To my amazement everybody kept saying nice things about me. Nearly all the speakers including Cheryl did so and I genuinely tried to play it down. As I said to one of my guests: "It is obviously 'be nice to Tony evening'". I should have known better: it was not to last.

De-blogged and resignations

Although not stated as one of the Club's objectives I had always hoped that the Blue Dragon Club might provide an opportunity for supporters to express their views on Welsh politics. I had been having some success with the co-founding and weekly blogging on a site called 'Enterprise Britain'.

Early in February 2010 I posted a 'blog' on the Club website. It was designed to attract comment. It was headed "Resignation: the weak option?" and discussed the defection of a North Wales County Councillor from the Conservatives to Plaid Cymru.

At the same time Caroline Oag updated the website with a report about the 2009 dinner including selected photographs of the attendees.

Without any reference to me the Welsh Conservative Office in Cardiff closed down the website. They did not like my blog and thought that the photographs of the dinner showed Conservatives to be 'toffs' and this could lose the Party votes.

It lost me Caroline and Sarah both of whom immediately resigned from the Committee.

However the General Election was nearing and I did not want to take any action which might be seen as counter-productive to the Welsh Conservatives. I spoke to a number of the Committee members and we were agreed on our compliant position.

The General Election came and went and Cheryl became Secretary of State for Wales. On Monday 19 July I visited Cardiff and had lunch with Caroline and Sarah. I would like to think that it was down to the Drury charm but their agreement to rejoin the Committee was more likely reflective of their commitment to Welsh politics.

I will not drink to that

On Thursday 17 December 2007 I stopped drinking – alcohol that is. On that day I was in the chair of pain in Leighton Buzzard having a tooth extracted.

"F*** me, that's a f****** great cavity" exclaimed my South African dentist as he completed a session of tugging and pulling. He showed me the offending molar as he wiped the sweat off his brow. He then explained that as it was nearing Christmas, and he was due to catch a plane at Heathrow and fly home, he proposed prescribing a five day course of antibiotics as a precautionary measure.

"And no f******* alcohol, Man. They are f****** strong pills. Got it? No f****** drinking."

The intake of alcohol had always been part of my life. The conviviality at St. Helen's Capital was based, in part, on our frequentation of a wine bar in London Wall.

After rising at 5.00am and catching the 6.05am into Euston, the Northern Line tube to Moorgate, the walk to Bishopsgate to start work at just after 7.00am, a glass (or two) of Merlot at lunchtime seemed right.

We often met professional colleagues and on occasions took our clients with us. Running enterprising businesses is not only hard work but also an occasionally solitary existence. We found that the relaxed nature of the wine bar and the effect of red wine allowed people to express themselves. It was at the heart of our success in that our clients became our friends. We had a high level of customer loyalty at St. Helen's Capital.

For me, however, the downside of this approach was a propensity to drink during the evening. As the years progressed I became vulnerable to wine and stress leading to over-reactions. All too often I sent emails late at night which I regretted the next day.

When I reflected on certain events at South West Bedfordshire Conservative Association I realised I had let myself down. I most certainly could have handled my decision to resign as a Bedfordshire County Councillor in a more constructive way. Councillor Angela Roberts tried to reason that she could work things out for me but I was too arrogant to listen.

At the point in time of hearing the alcoholic strictures from my dentist I had been wondering if alcohol was becoming too much of a driver in my life. I realised that I was planning the daily schedule to ensure I would be near a wine bar around 6.00pm in the evening.

After completing the five day course of antibiotics and not drinking alcohol, I wrote down my likely consumption of wine, lager and scotch over the Christmas and New Year period. I asked myself if I wanted to know what 2008 might hold for me if I did not drink. I did, I didn't and I haven't since.

If I am ever congratulated on my show of inner strength (quite often by people who, themselves, are heavy drinkers) I immediately explain that it is a demonstration of my weak personality. It is my inability to moderate my alcoholic intake that has necessitated the drastic action of not drinking at all.

The benefits did not come all at once. A good friend, John Bridges, who is a respected Corporate Financier in the City (and who worked with me at St. Helen's Capital), is a former self-confessed alcoholic. He took an immediate interest in my resolve and he spent many months talking to me. It is not easy.

After the initial explosion of self-esteem you start to struggle to rationalise why you gave up alcohol in the first place. Then you simply miss it.

On many Friday evenings I would wander up to Milton Keyes to have an end of week drink with my stockbroker. Michael MacDougall, who was an invitee at the Blue Dragon dinner on 2 December 2010, loves a glass of Merlot and my pot of tea somehow seems misplaced.

For some years I suffered from gout. After a year of non-drinking it disappeared. I lost a stone in weight. Most of all, I did not send emails out at 10.00pm. My personal relationships seem to have improved.

The Annual Dinner 2010

Thus, having made the decision not to renew my membership of the Conservative Party, I thought carefully, in fact very carefully, about my intended resignation as Chairman of the Blue Dragon Club. I knew that the annual dinner would cost me between £3,000 and £4,000 and I was not prepared to give Dave another penny. I therefore decided to argue that my increasing work commitments in the UK and in China were likely to make it difficult for me to continue. This was true.

In fact it was especially true because in the last quarter of 2010 trading at my corporate finance house improved and a trip to Hong Kong and Beijing in November proved successful.

I knew that it was not the real reason I was resigning but it was convincing. I was determined to go quietly and not damage the Club in any way.

On 15 September 2010 I wrote privately to Simon Baynes and explained the position to him. As I expected he was supportive and constructive and almost immediately he secured the agreement of Simon Mort to be Acting Chairman. I breathed a sigh of relief.

On 20 September 2010 Simon emailed me and said:

"....the Board this afternoon wanted me to express our profound thanks for all that you have done and to say that we would like to mark your Chairmanship with a special presentation whenever appropriate."

I replied by thanking Simon and the Board and pointing out that when my political views, (about which I had informed Simon), which were being expressed in private letters and more publicly in my blogs on 'Enterprise Britain', were known by the Conservatives more generally, I might find my presentation withdrawn.

On the same day Simon emailed again and said;

"There will be no change to our gratitude and respect for you and we would like very much to make the presentation to you at the BD Dinner which, after all, is open to non-members of the Conservative Party..."

On 21 September 2010 Simon wrote to the Blue Dragon Committee members about the dinner and carefully, without fuss, mentioned that I was stepping down as Chairman and that Simon Mort was taking over as Chairman. Simon wrote:

"I would like to thank Tony...on behalf of the Blue Dragon Committee and all the Welsh Conservatives for the fantastic job he has done as Chairman (he will be at the dinner...)"

Catrin Edwards, the Chairman of the Welsh Conservatives wrote publicly:

"We all owe Tony a huge debt of gratitude for the enormous amount of work that he has put in to driving the Blue Dragon forward..."

That evening I wrote to the Committee Members to thank them for all their hard work and support. I ended my email by saying: *"Cofion gorau am y dyfodol".*

My friend Richard Hopkin had stopped playing Chopin and translated into Welsh: *"I wish you all well for the future"*

In truth I had real reservations about attending the dinner on 2 December 2010. I was happy to pay £900 for a table (which I did) but I had succeeded in slipping away without affecting the work of the Club. I felt a presentation was not necessary.

On 23 September Councillor Jeff James emailed me:

"During your period in office I feel we made great progress and established a pattern for the future success of the Club."

On 27 September 2010 Simon Mort emailed me:

"Yours will be impossible boots to fill...We all look forward to seeing you on 2 December."

On 28 October 2010 I received an official letter from Catrin Edwards on behalf of the Welsh Conservatives.

I had received a personal letter from Simon Baynes dated 1 October 2010. It was generous in its comments. There was no choice. I had to attend the dinner.

Two days before the dinner I had an email from Sally. "You are coming?" she asked.

The evening of Thursday 2 December 2010 was awful. It was cold and it had been snowing. A number of the Welsh people, including Catrin Edwards, were unable to reach Paddington Station. Three people from my table cried off but it proved relatively easy to replace them. This is partly because amongst my City group Cheryl Gillan had become a respected speaker.

On reflection I now realise that something was wrong. I met Simon Mort early on and he was busy. Paul Stafford QC came up and apologised for not writing to me. We discussed meeting up.

Most of my attention was on my table guests and their arrival. I had written to them to mention that I was receiving a presentation and if they could not face hearing nice things about me they should leave the room. There was a certain amount of banter.

The main speeches took place before the dinner itself as the main speaker Professor Brian Griffiths wanted to speak early and Cheryl Gillan announced she had to leave early. There were five speeches.

I held my notes tightly.

Cheryl left and the dinner was served, Simon raised lots of money from the auction, the raffle prizes were distributed and finally Simon announced there was to be a presentation. I again gripped my papers and watched as Sally Dyson received some flowers for her work in organising the evening.

And that was that. Several of my guests realised that I was stunned. One told me to forget it.

I drove Michael MacDougall back to Milton Keynes and then I went home.

Before Christmas I received a Christmas card from The Welsh Conservative Party. It said:

"Thank you for all your work with the Blue Dragon Club."

The letter from Catrin Edwards, Chairman of the Welsh Conservative Party, dated 28 October 2010

I wonder who....

Is it possible that late in the day somebody decided that I should not receive a presentation. That is fine. I was pleased by the emails and letters I had received. What mattered most to me was that I had done a good job. I was happy with the comments I had received. I did not want a presentation and I would have been comfortable if Simon Baynes, or perhaps Simon Mort, had contacted me and said that, on balance, it was thought best if I did not attend.

But the way the Blue Dragon Club handled events surprised me. I wondered if the Committee Members were comfortable. My Christmas card from the Welsh Conservatives suggests it did not originate there.

Perhaps somebody wanted to make a point.

Postscript

At a later stage I decided that it was unfair to write the above without giving the Blue Dragon senior members a chance to comment. I wrote a polite note pointing out I had been snubbed. I received a rather wordy, and friendly, response. It explained that because of operational issues they could not fit in my presentation. They offered me alternatives to meet with them. I replied and thanked them but suggested we should move on.

Simon Mort, the Acting Chairman, again pressed me to meet and said "In any case, a present to indicate – for it can do no more – the great debt of gratitude which the Blue Dragon Club owes you is on its way."

The Chatham House Rule

On Tuesday 8 February 2011 I was entertained to lunch at the Carlton Club in St. James's by Simon Baynes and Simon Mort. We agreed the 'Chatham House Rule' would apply.

Chatham House, which was founded in 1920, is based in St. James's Square, Mayfair and is a prominent source of independent analysis and ideas on the building of a prosperous and secure world.

The Chatham House Rule, which was devised in 1927, and since revised, is:

"When a meeting, or part thereof, is held under the Chatham House Rule, participants are free to use the information received,

but neither the identity nor the affiliation of the speaker(s), nor that of any other participant, may be revealed."

We enjoyed a robust conversation on what was a delightful occasion. It reminded me of how much I was already missing the fellowship of the political spectrum.

I received my presentation: two interesting books on Wales and some 'Blue Dragon' decorated plates. It was reassuring to finish on a convivial note although I still wonder what happened on the night of the dinner.

VI - David Cameron, Andrew Mackay and Julie Kirkbride

For the Conservative Party, and its Constituency members, the years marking the end of Mrs. Thatcher's period in office, and the struggles of her successor, were testing. Despite John Major's remarkable election victory in 1992 (which allowed the eventual rise of Tony Blair) the period up to the General Election of 1997 were fraught.

In Chapter Four I mentioned the difficulties faced by the Chancellor of the Exchequer and the eventual fall of Norman Lamont. The European question caused David Madel huge problems in South West Bedfordshire. I can recall one meeting during this time, in Dunstable, when I thought that fighting might break out between the members.

Foreplay

It is reflective of a certain 'right to rule' within the Conservative hierarchy that wiped out the election, and the arrival of Tony and Cherie Blair in Downing Street, failed to bring home the reality of the situation.

A few weeks after the 1997 Election South West Bedfordshire held its annual dinner. The guest speaker was John Major. I recall sitting quietly as he seemingly dismissed the result as a 'one-off'. He suggested that the Conservative party was the greatest political body ever seen in the Western democratic territories.

By the time that William Hague had come, lost and gone and IDS had come, dithered, and gone and Michael Howard came, lost and resigned, even the most diehard Conservative was beginning to realise that there was a problem. The Party did not have a leader and lacked any sort of coherent manifesto. The sacking of Howard Flight during the 2005 Election campaign illustrated clearly that Campaign Headquarters was full of losers.

It was on 1 September 2005 that I realised the Messiah might be amongst us. On the day 'The Times' published an editorial article by a certain David Cameron. I had heard the name and the rumblings.

His article, which is shown below, was titled *'Where is the most civilised place on earth?'* and sub-titled *'It could be Britain. And if I become Conservative leader, I can see a route towards achieving that quality of life'*. It was about Inner City regeneration and preserving the countryside. The beginnings of 'The Big Society' ("...I want to see a new generation of visionary civil leaders..."). It was all summed up in the phrase "...modern compassionate Conservatism."

I was seduced by Cameron's rhetoric. I studied him carefully by reading and researching all the material I could. I asked every Conservative I met if they knew him. I listened to all the opinions that were offered. I took a keen interest in Samantha Cameron. I thought she was fabulous and I could see her striding the world stage.

I had read Hillary Clinton's autobiography 'Living History' which was published in 2003. She had received a $8m advance and it sold one million copies in the first month. Throughout she referred to "Bill Clinton": never "Bill" or "my husband". I thought it was inspirational and I remain disappointed that she did not gain the Democratic nomination for the 2009 Presidential election. She remains a World figure.

I also read Cherie Blair's autobiography 'Speaking for Myself' published in 2008. It is an enjoyable jaunt and written by an obviously intelligent person. But she's not Hillary Clinton!
I thought about the backing that Hillary gave to Bill and its importance to him. I felt that Samantha Cameron might offer the same for David.

I put a copy of 'The Times' article on the desks of all my colleagues. I wrote beneath the printed words; *"If you are interested in politics the above article in today's 'The Times' is well worth reading. David Cameron is my tip to become Conservative leader."*

Where is the most civilised place on Earth?

It could be Britain. And if I become Conservative leader, I can see a route towards achieving that quality of life

DAVID CAMERON

[Article text from The Times]

Handwritten note:
IF YOU ARE INTERESTED IN POLITICS THE ABOVE ARTICLE IN TODAY'S "THE TIMES" IS WELL WORTH READING. DAVID CAMERON IS MY TIP TO BECOME CONSERVATIVE LEADER.

TONY
1.9.05

The article in "The Times" on 1 September 2005 which brought David Cameron to my attention.

Consummation

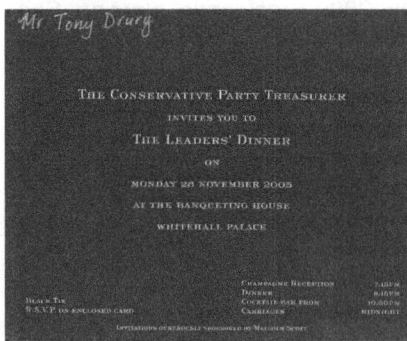

The Leaders' Dinner at which David Cameron visited our table.

Before long David Cameron and David Davis were locked in battle to become the next Conservative leader. Cameron's campaign brochure which spearheaded his battle for member votes contained the following sentence:

"I want to win support from Labour and Liberal Democrat voters...."

On 28 November 2005 I hosted a St. Helen's Capital table at 'The Leaders' Dinner' held at the Banqueting House, Whitehall Palace, London.

At the Leaders Dinner you are able to invite a Member of Parliament to be a guest on your table. I selected Nadine Dorries from Mid-Bedfordshire. One of my guests was so smitten with her that I maintained a close watch on developments. She went on to attract controversy over her Parliamentary expenses and an involvement with a married man.

During the evening David Cameron and David Davis completed their election campaigns. Their final speeches were contrasting in their style and content. David Cameron was the Leader in waiting and David Davis wasn't.

The future Conservative leader came to our table. He gave Nadine Dorries a smile and a wink. I introduced him to my guests. He really does know how to make an impact. It was electrifying.

One of my guests was a Chinese entrepreneur who fell over himself trying to extract his camera from his pocket. I afterwards told him that David Cameron had asked to meet him. He has been living on that story ever since. I really should have been a politician.

Front Bench Club Lunch
with The Rt.Hon. David Cameron
MOSIMANN'S
London

Marinated Scottish Salmon
Pickled Ginger, Lemongrass Vinaigrette
~oOo~
Roast Tournedos of Angus Beef
with Red Wine Shallot Sauce
Market Vegetables
~oOo~
Anton's Bread and Butter Pudding
~oOo~
Coffee
Petits Fours

Mosimann's Bourgogne Chardonnay 2004
Château Le Oume de Pey Médoc 1999

Tuesday 9th May 2006

Lunch with David Cameron 9 May 2006

Following his succession to leadership I seemed to meet David Cameron on a regular basis. At the time I was a member of the Front Bench Club (£5,000pa) and on 9 May 2006 lunched with him at Mosimann's. He later came as my guest to the reception for the Globalisation Institute which I discussed in Chapter Four.

The Blue Dragon Club was now evolving and I was to learn from Cheryl Gillan the support he was giving to the Welsh Conservatives.

Divorce

During 2006 and 2007 I was diverted by my departure from St. Helen's Capital and the onset of the recession. I began to lose several of my non-executive directorships and was involved in a desperate, and regrettably, unsuccessful attempt, to save one of my companies from collapsing. Despite several tense meetings I could not persuade the main investor to make a modest further share purchase without which other Funds would not commit. Finally the Bank became nervous. It went into receivership and it was my first ever 'failure'. It hurt. I lost my investment and unpaid salary of around £40,000. This was the time of the Blair/Brown succession and the world financial crisis.

By early 2009 I was having doubts about the direction that David Cameron was following. The Notting Hill set were gaining publicity and the name of Steve Hilton was becoming more familiar. Much more worrying was the lack of a clear manifesto. It was difficult because, if the Conservative's made a policy statement, Labour immediately assumed the merits and debunked the rest.

During the 2010 campaign two events disturbed me. The first was a breakfast organised by the Non-Executive Director's Association where the guest was David Willetts. I thought he was a key Conservative strategist. After he had given his speech, little of which stayed in the memory, I asked him the following question:

"Mr. Willetts, I will shortly be campaigning in Leighton Buzzard for Andrew Selous. When I am asked, on the doorstep, what do the Conservatives stand for, what is the answer?"

Nobody on the table at which I was seated understood his response.

A little later I attended a speech given by Michael Gove. This was organised in London by the Centre for Policy Studies ("CPS").

Michael spoke for a little over an hour. It was one of the most remarkable performances I have ever witnessed. Of course, the right wing Thatcherite audience loved it. It contained an avalanche of empirical data, global comparisons, gushing sentiments and a stream of policies.

I left the building (St. Stephen's Club in Mayfair) thinking that Michael Gove was rather frenzied. His performances to-date as a Cabinet Minister might suggest I had a point.

Coalition

Trevor Kavanagh, writing in 'The Sun' on 20 December 2010, said that *"David Cameron's failure to win was tantamount to defeat."*

I have always thought that we should have tried for minority Government. It was constitutionally quite viable.

Gordon Brown had said, prior to the election, that the Party with the most seats could have the first chance to form a Government. David Cameron should have accepted that position. Gordon Brown would have met with the Queen and Her Majesty would have invited David Cameron to form a Government.

Labour would have imploded and the Liberal Democrats (who lost five seats in the election) would do what they know best. They would have argued amongst themselves. Weeks of wrangling would have been saved. The Shadow Cabinet could have started work and Dave and George could have told us that there was a financial crisis and it was all Gordon Brown's fault.

Possibly the Government might have been defeated but I doubt if that would have happened for at least eighteen months. History shows that minority governments often win the next election. In Scotland, since 2007, the minority Scottish National Party has stayed in power for four years.

The subsequent formation of the Coalition Government and Cameron's toadying to the Liberal Democrats, with Nick Boles and the Notting Hill set screaming in delight, is a betrayal of everything I have believed in and worked for. The 1922 Committee is squirming in agony and are occasionally questioning the proposal of a joint manifesto in the assumed 2015 election. Cameron is walking all over them.

His arrogance is beyond belief. He is power crazed and already planning his own history. He takes his pals on trips to India and China which serve absolutely no purpose (forget the PR spin). He tells Pakistan to sort out its borders (does he have any idea what he talking about?) and he tells the EU to sort out its budgets.

His Etonian approach to being Prime Minister, his already frightening lack of consistency, his lack of grasp of economics and his bullying style does not bode well for the future.
The above represents a personal viewpoint. It led to my leaving the Conservative Party.

It was a decision that had other consequences.

Andrew Mackay

I first met the then Conservative Member of Parliament in 2005. He had been re-elected in that year with a majority of 12,036 and became MP for Bracknell in 1997. He had entered

Andrew Mackay (left) and myself on the 15th Green at Aberdovey Golf Course.

Parliament in 1983 for the then Berkshire East Constituency. From 1997 – 2001 he had been Shadow Secretary of State for Northern Ireland and had held a variety of other positions.

Andrew and his wife, Julie Kirkbride, the MP for Bromsgrove, were known as the 'Golden Couple'. In Andrew's case regular sessions under the sun lamp helped to maintain this aura.

During the removal of Howard Flight as an MP in the May 2005 election my understanding is that it was Andrew who visited Howard's Arundel and South Downs members and effectively laid down the law. As such he was working for the then leader Michael Howard and his Australian strategist Lynton Crosby. It was a sad time for Party democracy.

During a Blue Dragon reception in London, and before I became involved, I found myself talking to Andrew and we discovered that we both were members of Aberdovey Golf Club in Wales. He and Julie were (and still are) regular visitors.

Since that time we have played together on a regular basis. Andrew is an intensely competitive opponent. His golf swing reminds me of an agitated octopus with arms flying in all directions. But he is difficult to beat. I think our record is all square. Quite often Julie would walk round with us and I came to understand her passion for her work as a politician.

Andrew became a 'Special Adviser to the Leader of the Opposition Party'. Although he was clearly close to David Cameron he was always discreet. Unlike some of his other colleagues he was, however, interested in my point of view. He was enthusiastic about the development of the Blue Dragon Club.

During the Summer of 2006 I arranged for the Board of Directors (I was the UK Chairman) of Sunrise Biotech Holding Limited, a PLUS-quoted company based in Beijing, to visit the House of Commons and meet with Andrew. Yonghu Li, the Chairman, despite not speaking English, communicated enthusiastically with Andrew through the interpreter and we did our bit that day for Anglo-Chinese relationships.

MPs' Expenses

The world of Andrew Mackay and Julie Kirkbride was to come crashing down during the MPs' expenses scandal in 2009. After a contentious meeting with his constituents Andrew announced that he would stand down as a MP. Julie's story is told below.

During that time I remained in regular contact with Andrew often by text messaging and the occasional game of golf. After he resigned we had lunch together and I listened to his side of the story. Not that I sought to judge because I did not fully understand all the issues.

Following the 2010 General Election Andrew announced he was joining a PR agency: "After leaving Parliament I want to be a part of a winning team that is assisting global businesses face their strategic communications challenges and Burson-Marsteller provides a fantastic opportunity to do this." He had received a number of job offers because he remained in close contact with senior Conservatives. He almost certainly still had (and possibly has) access to the Prime Minister.

Andrew's position deteriorated following the publication of the October 2010 report from the Standards Commissioner. John Lyons examined whether Andrew acted within the rules in identifying as his main home the Bromsgrove property he shared with Julie. Mr Lyons concluded:

"Mr Andrew Mackay breached the rules relation to second home allowances...We are very disappointed that, even after seeing the Commissioner's full report, Mr. Mackay maintains that he did not break the rules, when it is quite clear that he did. Mr. Mackay has already paid a high price for making such a serious misjudgement....He has also repaid a considerable sum of money..."

My final contact with Andrew was at the Blue Dragon reception on 7 September 2010 when he and Julie came as my guests. I had mentioned this to Cheryl Gillan early in the day when we had lunch: "Will the press be there?" she had asked. Shortly afterwards we had the lunch at Wiltons with Michael Howard that Andrew organised for me.

On Monday 20 September 2010 I wrote to Andrew (and Julie) to tell him that I was not renewing my membership of the Conservative Party. He wrote back:

"I formed a very favourable view of David during my four years as his Senior Political and Parliamentary Adviser and believe he will be an outstanding Prime Minister."

Andrew concluded by saying:

"Keep in touch and hopefully you might rejoin us soon."

That is unlikely to happen. I hope that we might play golf together again.

Julie Kirkbride

Julie suffered hideously during the MPs' expenses scandal and did not seek re-election in the 2010 General Election. She was accused of *"within the rules of the House in claiming interest on the increased mortgage she took out in order to build an additional bedroom in her home in Bromsgrove when it was used by her brother principally to assist her with childcare."*

In October 2010 the Standards Commissioner, John Lyons, did not uphold the complaint against her.

Three weeks after the General Election in 2010 Julie joined Tetra Strategy, a firm specialising in political lobbying.

Julie is rather attractive, and perhaps, unlike some of the other high profile 'lookers and dressers' in Westminster, she is tactile and warm. I began to know her quite well as she walked round the links at Aberdovey. Andrew takes ages to line up his putt and play the stroke. We therefore had time to talk. Julie was on the Trade and Industry Committee and we shared an interest in enterprising businesses.

The events at Bromsgrove meant that the Press had a 'field day' at her cost. The 'Daily Mail' of 25 July 2009 carried an article (including a photograph) with the heading 'Shamed Tory may stand at election'.

'The Sunday Times' on 18 April 2010 carried a wide-ranging article with the heading *"Shamed Tory bids to cash in on home"* and included pictures of Julie, Andrew and her Bromsgrove flat. Even a year later the press continued with their articles. 'The Times' on 1 December 2010 carried a picture of Julie with the sub-heading *"Ex-MP Julie Kirkbride spent taxpayers' money on a photoshoot for her website"*.

Julie joined Andrew in attending the Blue Dragon reception on 7 September 2010. The last time I saw her was at the Blue Dragon dinner on 2 December 2010. She became involved in handing out the raffle prizes and seemed radiant.

It is sometimes forgotten that events such as the MPs' expenses scandal put pressure on other people. Andrew and Julie added much to my time as a Conservative member. I never had a moment's doubt about rejecting the Coalition Government but it is frustrating that valued friendships have been affected.

The Future

That would appear to be the end of my political career. I have chosen not to continue as a member of the Conservative Party. I have wonderful memories and some good friends. I suppose I am floating.

David Cameron won't care. Since he became leader Party membership is thought to have fallen from 258,000 in 2005 to around 170,000. One more doesn't matter. He will prop up the coffers from his wealthy friends and put all his efforts to maintaining the Coalition Government so that in 2015 the anticipated revival of the economy will allow him to secure an election victory.

He will continue to walk all over many of the principles which have been the bedrock of Conservatism over the last fifty years. He will focus on power and personal prestige. Some of the Conservative back benchers will continue to act like sheep enjoying their fabulous earnings and life style. If they lose their seats they will have a great pension and a huge tax free pay-off.

In a YouGov poll for 'The Sunday Times' (3 April 2011) voters were asked to suggest who is the most irritating politician in the country. 48% of those asked found David Cameron fairly or very irritating.

Frankly, he worries the living daylights out of me.

I will satisfy my wish to contribute by blogging weekly on www.enterprisebritain.com.

VII - Enterprise Britain and Mr. Angry

I first met Dirk van Dijl, a Dutch American economist, in 2006. We worked together for a period of time and shared a common interest in trying to understand the component parts which might make up 'Enterprise Britain'.

Dirk is an inspirational character. We started www.enterprisebritain.com a little over two years ago. Under his management and leadership it now has over sixteen bloggers and a growing audience.

I have settled down to providing a weekly blog. A few weeks ago I was fuming about the state of the roads in my local community. On a Sunday evening I was blogging away in exasperation at the potholes and suddenly Mr. Angry was (re)born. He seemed able to better express my frustrations.

After several weeks of blogging in my own right, and in my alter ego, Dirk suggested that I split the blog into two. I discussed matters with Mr. Angry who, of course, had to take instructions from Mrs. Angry.

Now each week on a Sunday evening I write my blog and try to contain Mr. Angry as he lashes out at the injustices he perceives in our society. He doesn't like David Cameron, Vince Cable, bankers, Revenue and Customs inspectors, EU law makers and all those sycophantic Cameron disciples who rush up to the PM and proclaim the words 'entrepreneur', 'enterprise' and 'Coalition'.

Earlier in 'Goodbye Dave' I mentioned that I gave up drinking alcohol in December 2007. I therefore read with interest a first person article in 'The Times' (11 August 2010) written by Debbie Perriss. She explained how she and her family had held together during her husband's fight with alcoholism.

I met with Colin Perriss and we have become friends. He is developing a business using his personal experience and research into understanding and managing what is a national problem. We discussed a blog and now Colin is delivering a weekly contribution to www.enterprisebritain.com Dirk is reporting that he has a growing readership.

I am afraid that Mr. Angry is beyond help but I suspect Colin may influence many business people before he is finished.

I invite you to join Enterprise Britain and hope you enjoy the blogs.

Index

A

Alex Singleton, 44, 45
Alexander Boris de Pfeffel Johnson, 15
Andrew Date, 25
Andrew Mackay, 16, 36, 37, 43, 63, 69, 71
Andrew Neil, 33, 34
Andrew Selous, 15, 16, 21, 22, 23, 24, 25, 32, 33, 67
Angela Roberts, 5, 7, 26, 27, 32, 55
    Peter Roberts, 26
Ann Widdecombe, 35
Ashley Mote, 22

B

Bernard Gentry, 50
Bill Clinton, 64

C

Caroline Oag, 49, 53
Catrin Edwards, 19, 49, 57, 58
Cherie Blair, 63, 64
Cheryl Gillan, 11, 12, 13, 19, 51, 52, 53, 54, 58, 59, 67, 71
Colin Perriss, 75, 76

D

Damien Green, 45
David Cameron, 6, 9, 10, 11, 12, 13, 14, 15, 18, 20, 36, 37, 42, 43, 44, 45, 47, 51, 56, 63, 64, 65, 66, 67, 68, 69, 70, 73, 74, 75
David Davis, 34, 65, 66
David Jones, 12, 13
David Madel, 6, 21, 22, 32, 63
David Mellor, 21
David Rowland, 9
David Willetts, 67
Debbie Perriss, 75
Dirk van Dijl, 75, 76
Dr. Paul Stafford, 50, 59

E

Eric Pickles, 45
Evan Price, 50

G

George Osborne, 17, 42
Gladstone, 15
Gordon Brown, 39, 68

H

Harold Macmillan, 15
Havard Hughes, 50
Hillary Clinton, 64
Hobhouse, 5

I

Iain Duncan Smith, 24, 30, 31, 45

J

Jeff James, 49, 58
Jeremy Paxman, 35
Jin Jin Leune, 17, 18
John Bridges, 55
John Howard, 35
John Lyons, 71, 72
John Major, 6, 38, 39, 63
John Reid, 43
Jonathan Evans, 12
Julie Kirkbride, 16, 46, 63, 70, 71, 72, 73

K

Kenneth Clarke, 30
Kirstie Williams, 52

L

Lady Thatcher, 21, 30
Lindsay Jenkins, 22
Lord Broughton, 5
Lord Howard Flight, 36, 38, 41, 42, 43, 44, 45, 46, 47, 63, 70
Lord Howe of Aberavon, 37
Lord Hunt of Wirral, 53
Lord Lamont of Lerwick, 38
Lord Peter Walker, 16, 36, 37
Lord Young of Grantham, 47
Lynton Crosby, 35, 36, 70

M

Mark Warde-Norbury, 40, 47
Michael Gove, 68
Michael Howard, 16, 30, 32, 34, 35, 36, 37, 42, 43, 63, 70, 72
Michael MacDougall, 19, 56, 59

N

Nadine Dorries, 66
Neville Bowman-Shaw, 6, 25
Nicholas Littlewood, 17
Nick Boles, 10, 11, 69
Nick Bourne, 12, 49, 52
Nick Clegg, 5, 22, 52
Nick Herbert, 43
Nigel Horton, 20
Norman Lamont, 38, 39, 40, 41, 45, 47, 63

P

Peter Hain, 11, 52
Peter Stringfellow, 34
Philip Rose, 5

R

Rhodri Morgan, 11
Richard Hopkin, 50, 58

Robert Boot, 4, 11, 16
Robert Harvey, 45, 48
Robert John, 52
Robert Walpole, 15
Ruth Lea, 39, 40, 41

S

Sally Dyson, 50, 59
Sandra Howard, 36
Sarah Timothy, 49
Simon Baynes, 49, 50, 56, 58, 60, 61
Simon Heffer, 45
Simon Mort, 17, 50, 53, 57, 58, 59, 60, 61
Sir Alex Douglas-Home, 15
Sir Anthony Eden, 15
Sir Paul Stevenson, 45
Sir Peter Brown, 6
Steve Hilton, 10, 67

T

Tom Wise, 21, 22, 25
Tony Blair, 21, 24, 25, 30, 63
Trevor Kavanagh, 68

W

William Hague, 24, 30, 31, 32, 63
William Pitt the Elder, 15

www.ingramcontent.com/pod-product-compliance
Lightning Source LLC
Chambersburg PA
CBHW071329040426
42444CB00009B/2116